A WOUNDED WOMAN WAITING ON HER MATE

How to overcome dysfunctional relationships so that you can meet and marry the man of your dreams

Elishia Dupree

WRITE WAY PUBLISHING, LLC.
7302 Wesley Providence Parkway
Lithonia, GA 30038

This book is available online at Amazon.com

ISBN 978-0-9916687-0-0
ISBN Ebook: 978-0-9916687-1-7

DEDICATION

This book is dedicated to my tests, trials, processes and pains. I thank God for using my dirt to help me to grow into a beautiful garden and to discover that there are far too many women in the world who are disappointed, angry and bitter in their quests to find Mr. Right. The practical insights in this book are designed to help women look deeply inside their pain and move purposefully toward wholeness. God loves His daughters and wants nothing but the best for His girls.

CONTENTS

ACKNOWLEDGEMENTS

I would like first to acknowledge Jesus Christ, my Lord and Saviour. Without Him, I can do nothing. I am so grateful to be called a friend of God. Second, I would like to acknowledge my four children who allowed me to take time from them to complete this book. Special thanks to Daphnee McDonald and my nephew, Qualan McDonald, for the times that they cooked and cared for the children while I was typing away. I also would like to acknowledge my mother and father who have gone on to be with the Lord. I am what I am today because of the things they poured into me. Special thanks to my spiritual father and mother Apostle Travis and Stephanie Jennings of The Harvest Tabernacle Church, Atlanta, Georgia; my former pastors, Apostle Mario and Prophetess Pamela Kimball, Lion of Judah Family Worship Center, Riverdale, Georgia, who were major participants in my spiritual growth and healing. My gratitude to Lorestine Pittman, my editor, for her diligence with the book's content and Bobby Barnhill, my graphic designer, for his creative genius in the book's presentation.

Chapter 1

INTRODUCTION

If you picked up this book, that means you are somewhat interested in the title and its contents. You are hopeful that it will address the thoughts that are going through your mind, e.g., "Why am I not married yet?" "Why can't I find the right man?" "Is there something wrong with me?" These questions are addressed in this book, "A Wounded Woman Waiting on Her Mate," but you will have to take a journey within to find the root cause(s) of and answer(s) to some of your relationship problems.

This book will help you to stop blaming others for your relationship woes and cause you to evaluate yourself by honestly responding to and completing the self-assessments included at the end of each chapter. Being transparent with yourself is the initial step on the journey within to break up your fallow ground and prepare for a bountiful relationship.

Too much time is spent fostering relationships that are doomed from the start. You know what I mean. I have discovered that each individual has his or her own perception or definition of what is a relationship. Therefore, when meeting a person on a personal basis, it is most important firstly to know your perception or definition of what a relationship is and, secondly, what they think a relationship is. If their definition doesn't line up with yours, to proceed would be a waste of your time and theirs. Several scenarios of real-life situations are detailed below. Please read them and be prepared to complete the self-assessment at the end of the chapter.

Scenario A: When you first meet him, you immediately size him up and you think he is cute. And because you are available, you are wide open to the "possibilities." He tells you a couple of things that make you feel good because you haven't heard them in a while, and you might even fall for them. He talks to you all night so that he can gather information about what type person you are. You share personal information with him hoping that he is the one -- the good candidate for marriage. Then, the first red flag comes when he tells you something like, I'm married but my wife and I have been separated for five years.

The brake light comes on and you are like, "What?" But you downplay what you heard and start to think that maybe this still can work. You like his conversation. He likes yours. You all have created some type of chemistry and could be headed in the right direction as soon as he gets rid of this wife.

Well, it's not that simple. There is a reason why he has not gotten rid of the wife. It's been five years and he has not filed for divorce! Because you are desperate, you overlook that sign of trouble. Then he tells you, "I have five children from her. I don't want to get a divorce because she will kill me with child support."

By this time, you are all the way in and you start to feel sorry for him in his situation. The mercy part of you will enable his foolish behavior, and you become a team player in this adulterous affair. He makes himself look as if he's the victim. And you take the bait. Now you are into something that you did not bargain for.

Five months into the relationship and he still has not filed for divorce, but he introduces the kids to you. Wow, isn't this exciting!

You have even had some choice words with the wife. What have you gotten yourself into? In the beginning all you wanted was a loving relationship but you never knew it would come to this. Your emotions are all tied up and you have suggested to him that you would pay for the divorce.

To your surprise, he doesn't take the offer. He says, "I'm a man and I will handle it myself." He could handle it but there's just one problem: He lost his job a month ago. Now he's receiving unemployment and barely making ends meet. He's stressed and so are you because you want to be married NOW. You back up from the relationship and give him an ultimatum: It's you or her! You tell him that you are not going to sit around and wait for him to drag this situation out. You are frustrated and fuming mad. You're gaining weight and your face is breaking out in big pimples. What went wrong? Is it his or your fault that you are in this state?

Scenario B: You have been single and celibate for some time and all of your girlfriends seem to be getting married. Every time you go to their weddings, you are the one who catches the bouquet. It's been four years but there is no sign of a healthy relationship in sight. Your girlfriends introduce you to a mutual friend of theirs and you go out on a date. The guy is nice looking, he smells good, and is a perfect gentleman. You are excited and enjoying the night because you haven't been out in a while.

He takes you to dinner at one of the nicest restaurants in town. When he opens his wallet, you notice all types of credit cards and a large amount of cash. You are getting more excited because, finally, you have met a man who can hold his own. After dinner, he wants to take you on a walk downtown. While you all are walking, he starts to share about his career and personal hobbies. You notice that he's a well-rounded man. That's a plus in your potential mate check box.

He walks you to your car and makes sure you get inside before he closes the door. You tell him thank you, and that you enjoyed the night. He says he enjoys everything about you. You begin to blush and tell him to call you in the morning. He calls you in the morning and you all chit-chat for a while. Then he asks to take you out for dinner again. You try to play hard to get by telling him you have a lot of homework to do. He says he understands. And since you have a lot of homework, why not let me drop off your dinner to you and get back with you in the morning? You take him up on his offer and tell him to come at 6:00 p.m.

The doorbell rings at 5:59 p.m. He's standing there with a nice leather jacket on and an outfit that brings out his soft brown complexion. He hands you a hot-seafood platter from a well-known restaurant and a bouquet of beautiful pink flowers wrapped with a bow. He gives you a hug that says, 'I am here for you.' He then tells you to call if you need him. He walks away. You are stunned because you can't believe that this guy is so romantic and understanding.

The night goes by and you are exhausted from your studies. Just as you are about to lie down, a text message comes through and it's him sending you a poem titled, "The Day I Laid my Eyes on You!" You are feeling some kind of way. You are not sure how to receive this. On Day 3, you call him to thank him for the food, flowers, and card. He says, "It was my pleasure." He starts to ask you questions about what you want out of life? Would you like to be married some day? You answer his questions but your answers are very vague. You are not sure where this is going so you try not to put too much into it.

He notices your apprehension and shifts the conversation to make you laugh. As you begin to laugh, you start to loosen up and share a little about your ambitions, hopes, and desires. He listens the entire time and only interjects when you ask him to. You are thinking this has got to be husband material because he seems to be so interested in what matters to you. The doorbell rings. There is a delivery guy at the door with an edible arrangement with a note that reads, "Will you go out with me on Friday at 7:00 p.m. at the Ritz-Carlton Hotel? You are still on the phone with him when he asks, was there someone at the door? You respond, yes, there was a delivery guy with an edible arrangement and an invitation. He says, well, do you accept my invitation?

You thank the delivery guy and shut the door in amazement. After what seems like five minutes, you respond by saying, of course. You ask what the dress code is. He says look deep down in the bag the guy left. You reach down and pull out this beautiful, sexy, sleeveless dress with Rhinestones gathering the front. You are speechless at this point! He says, hello. You say, yes. Then you ask him how he knew what size dress you wore. How did he know you had shoes to match the dress? He says I used to be a designer for women so I'm very familiar with shapes and sizes. The first date you went on I admired your shoes and found the perfect dress to match those shoes. You say, Why are you doing all of this? He says I just know what I want and what I want just happens to be you.

With a little fear in your tone, you say, "You don't even know me yet." He says, I know your heart and that's all I need to know. To make a long story short, after two months of dating, you become intimate. He continues to pursue you but you back away from the relationship because of the shame of fornication. He is devastated and doesn't understand why you won't answer his calls. Eventually, you answer his telephone call and tell him that you think you all need to stop spending time together. He is not in agreement and begins to stalk you. You eventually have to get a restraining order and fear being home alone. What went wrong? Who's to blame?

Scenario C: You just got your divorce after 10 years of marriage. The divorce ended very bitterly with lots of unmet needs, unresolved issues, and unhealed hurts on your part. You promised yourself you would never get into that situation again. One day while at work, the overnight shipping delivery man comes by and starts talking a little longer than he normally does. He asks, where's your ring? You say, oh, I'm not married any more. He says, well it must be my turn now. Blushing you say, "Boy, I am not trying to get into any more relationships. I'm trying to find myself." He says, jokingly, 'don't deny yourself love because of one man's mistake.' You look up in amazement and agree that he's right. He asks for your number; you give it to him. He says he will call you at 9:00 p.m. He calls you at 9:00 and asks if he can come over. You respond favorably.

He comes over to your house and you have cooked a full course meal for him. He eats with enjoyment and tells you that he didn't know you could cook like that. Your children come home from a high school football game. They get this total look of surprise on their faces when they see there is a man in their house whom they have never met and he is eating dinner. You introduce the man to your children and send them to the back of the family room. He asks how many kids do you have? You tell him you have three. Shortly after dinner, you ask him if he would like to watch a movie. He says, sure.

You ask him if he drinks wine, and he says, yes. While you all are watching the movie, you pour him a glass of wine. You both begin to drink and you start telling him about your marriage. He listens to your story and assures you that your ex-husband has lost out on a good thing.

He begins to get sleepy and asks if he can lie down on your couch until morning. You think about it, then tell him, yes, since you have known him for two years at the job. You bring blankets and pillows to him on the couch. He falls sound asleep. He wakes up about five o'clock in the morning and knocks on your bedroom door. You open the door and come out to see him out of the house. He tells you thanks for dinner and the movie. He kisses you on your forehead; you give him a hug. Boy, do you miss being cuddled up at night with a strong handsome man. You wave goodbye as he gets into his car.

Your daughter heard you get up and asks, Momma, who was that man? You answer, just a co-worker. Go back to sleep. You are excited about having a man around again. It's like a breath of fresh air. You said to yourself that you didn't want a relationship, but it felt good having someone to share your thoughts with.

It's about 2:00 p.m. and the overnight shipping delivery guy shows up. You rush to put on your lipstick and check to make sure your hair is in tip-top shape. He sees you and compliments you on how nice your hair looks today. You tell him, thank you, and ask, "So when am I going to see you again?" He says soon because he loves your cooking. You invite him over to dinner on the weekend. He tells you he has a ball game to attend with his son on Saturday but he will come by on Sunday after church.

You start preparing for Sunday on Thursday. You go out and get the best Sunday meal the local grocer has to offer. You clean the house and get fresh candles and flowers. The kids have agreed to go over to their dad's house for the weekend -- leaving you to have the house all to yourself. You are singing and dancing again and have told all your girlfriends about this fine man at work who you think is a good candidate to date. They encourage you to go shopping so you can be ready for this date and not look like a divorcee. You go and get some tight jeans, nice boots, and the best perfume on the market. You are ready. You are looking and smelling good.

He shows up at the house empty-handed with his work clothes on. You greet him with a kiss and he greets you back by hitting you on the butt. He says, Oooo, Wee. It smells good in here. What are you cooking? You say it's for me to know and for you to find out. You sit him down at the table and ask him to close his eyes. He closes his eyes and you put a plate of beautiful southern fried chicken, bowls of collard greens and potato salad, and sweet potato pie, on the table before him. He opens his eyes to see this magnificent meal and he is so excited. As you all are conversing over dinner, he starts to share his child support issue with you. He says, if he doesn't pay his child support, he's going to go to jail and lose his job. You ask him how much he is in arrears.   He says, just $2,000.00. He asks if you can loan the money to him, which he will repay to you in a month. You agree, but not before explaining that this is the only savings that you have and that you really need it back. He agrees that he will pay it back and assures you that you will see him every day. You go into your wallet and write out a check to him in the amount of $2,000.00.

After dinner, you turn on some relaxing music. You guys begin to slow jam -- his body next to yours and yours next to his. Before you know it, he spins you around and throws you onto the chair. He starts taking off your shirt. After he takes off your shirt, he begins to lick you from top to bottom. You avail yourself to him and the rest is history. He enjoys an afternoon of flaming hot sex with you. You beg him for more before realizing the lateness of the hour. It's 8:00 p.m. You tell him you are late picking up the kids and that he has to leave, but you will call him later on that night.

You don't have to call him because he calls you around 11:00 p.m. and tells you how good the sex was. You blush and tell him how great he made you feel. He talks to you for another hour and then he says those magic words, "I love you." You listen in silence and then tell him that you enjoyed the entire time you all shared. He whispers and says I'll see you tomorrow.

Monday afternoon, he didn't come by nor call. You thought that was weird because, for the last two years, he has always shown up at 2:00 p.m. You call him and his phone goes straight to voicemail. Now, you really are wondering what's going on. You check your bank account, the check has been cashed. You call him again. This time a girl picks up and says that the overnight shipping delivery guy is her fiancé. You are so upset that you want to strangle him. What went wrong? Who's to blame?

Every last one of these women was in different places in their lives. They all knew they wanted a mate but did not know that they are wounded. A wounded woman does not make sound decisions. Her decisions usually are out of her emotions. She ignores warning signs and gets caught up in the moment. Let's review the first chapter

What do you think about Scenarios A, B, and C? Have you experienced either Scenario? What was   the outcome?

_____

_____

_____

_____

_____

_____

_____

_____

What could each of the women have done differently?

_____

_____

_____

_____

_____

_____

_____

What are some of the women's strengths/weaknesses? What are your strengths/weaknesses?

_____

_____

_____

_____

_____

_____

What character traits did each woman exhibit? Is either woman similar to you?

_____

_____

_____

_____

_____

_____

Would you have done anything differently from what these women did? Why? Why not?

_____

_____

_____

_____

_____

_____

Chapter 2

WHO IS WOUNDED?

How do you know if you are wounded? I'm glad you asked. A wounded person struggles with feelings of anxiety, depression, anger, hurt, insecurity, neediness, emptiness, jealousy, fear, loneliness, misery, guilt, and shame. This person may appear to be cool, calm and collective but their behaviors will expose the pain. The first behavior is a lack of trust. Do you have problems trusting others? Do you believe what they tell you or do you find yourself suspecting that they are liars. Do you accuse others of being dishonest? If your answer is yes to any of the above questions you may have *trust issues*. Lack of trust can doom a relationship before it begins. The second example is criticism. Do you constantly criticize yourself or others? *Criticism* is destructive in relationships if it's used to devalue and not to enhance. When a person is critical of themselves most likely they will become critical of others.

The third is *anger.* Anger is a familiar response if you find yourself irritable and unable to control your emotions. If you tend to lash out on others, this is a problem that needs to be resolved. If anger is not dealt with or managed, it will only get worse. Fourth are *jealousy and envy*. They are like two bad cousins. They can destroy any good relationship before it gets started. If you have a problem with your mate interacting with the opposite sex, you might be too jealous. If you get mad when he compliments another woman or looks at another woman, you might be a little insecure.

Last is *defensiveness.* A defensive person is not receptive to receiving counsel, constructive criticisms or opinions. These types of people become very uneasy and possibly argumentative about the simple things in life. These are your drama queens. For example, if you become defensive when your mate tries to address something that you're not giving or doing, you may become impossible to deal with. People who are defensive usually misinterpret every word someone says and process them according to their negative messages. Communication with this person becomes difficult and frustrating. If you can relate to anything mentioned previously, you are wounded to some degree.

The symptoms of your pain is connected to a deeper hurt. Nothing just happens. Everything happens because something has caused it to happen. Consistently entering into bad relationships is symptomatic of a bigger problem. Many of our problems stem from childhood pain. Some psychologists theorize that a child who was neglected physically or emotionally tends to be either extremely needy or extremely defensive. He or she may exhibit clingy behavior and grow up to be a victim in his or her relationships or become emotionally distant with others including his or her own children.

Those who experience emotional abuse in childhood also are likely to find it difficult to develop intimate, healthy relationships as adults. Some have a difficult time connecting with their spouse. Others tend to suffer from extreme anxiety in dealing with the issues of rejection and abandonment. They may develop anti-social behaviors that further isolate them from relating to others. Rule number one is to acknowledge that you are wounded.

Once you have acknowledged the pain, the next step is to allow yourself to become open to the negative emotions. If you avoid your feelings, the pain will not go away. It will re-surface in other areas of your life. The most common area is relationship bonding. The Last step is to admit that the pain is there. These three elements are important to your healing. If you don't move forward, you will remain wounded. Wounded women subconsciously attract hurting men. These type of men are usually not good candidates for marriage. They prey on hurting women and take advantage of their vulnerabilities. It is best to deal with your pain now than to continue in dysfunctional relationships.

Women who avoid the pain of their past will most likely repeat the same destructive behaviors. You cannot heal what you refuse to confront. Confrontation is the key to your deliverance. No one wants to continue hurting. You deserve so much better than that. You can receive better relationships if you are ready to acknowledge, allow and admit.

After reading the above paragraphs, can you see how being wounded can destroy your personal lives and your ability to relate to others? It is a domino effect. Let's revisit one of the results of a woman entering into a relationship with her childhood pain. As stated in the beginning of the chapter, you can become very clingy. According to the Macmillan dictionary, the definition of clingy is a person wanting to be with another person all the time in a way that is annoying. If a man has to beg for space, that means he's not getting enough of it. A woman who misbehaves when her man does things alone is displaying signs of insecurity. No one wants to feel like they are being restricted. A healthy man loves a confident woman who has a life of her own. If a woman gives a guy the impression that she cannot function without him, he will automatically withdraw. A woman who has the characteristics of being mother hen, that is, smothering her man, will have a hard time receiving mutual love.

Here are a few things a woman does unaware in relationships. She tries so hard to love her man that she ends up smothering him instead. Signs of smothering can be 1) Neglecting her responsibilities and picking up his, 2) Forsaking her friendships in order to fit into his plans, 3) Catering to him hand and foot without any limits, and 4) Calling him too much and expecting him to call her several times a day. This may seem like love to her but it can be very misleading and a little annoying to her man. When a woman's existence depends on her being with a man, she will appear clingy, desperate, and unattractive.

Fear of abandonment may cause a woman to hold on too tightly. Earlier I spoke about the reasons a woman can exhibit clingy behavior. It usually stems from being neglected in childhood. Another reason she may hold on too tightly is the fear of losing something thought to be valuable. He may be valuable, but if she loses herself in the process, that's more devastating.

A woman with abandonment issues is usually controlled by fear. Fear drives her mental state of mind causing her to see stuff in her relationship that's not there at all. The anxiety of wanting her relationship to last can push her mate further away instead of drawing him closer. Is she a bad person? No, she is not at all. She's a good woman with issues. Unfortunately her partner has a hard time seeing the good stuff because her negative behaviors block his panoramic view. When fear drives a relationship, it is more controlled than developed. If a man feels like he's being controlled, he will automatically withdraw. This can lead to a downward spiral of loss.

If the need to be loved goes unfulfilled, a woman can spend a lifetime trying to fill the missing void in her soul. She will jump into relationship after relationship trying to fill that void in her life that was created during her childhood. I caution women to gain self-awareness before entering into a relationship. You must be healed on the inside before you can take on the challenges of being connected to another. The time you take to examine your life will be well worth the benefits. It will help you thrive and become fulfilled. Two years ago, I became aware of some of the reasons I continued to choose the wrong men. They are rooted in the relationship between my father and me. It's called the fatherless daughter syndrome.

Fatherless Daughter Syndrome

When I was born, my parents were very excited to receive their first girl into our family. My mother and father were recently married and now had three children. My mother had two boys prior to meeting my father. From the outside looking in, we were a happy blended family.

As the years went by, our family grew farther and farther apart. The awful life-altering drugs invaded our home. My father became addicted to crack and spent a lot of time in and out of prison. What once was family time was now spent in the streets and on drugs. All I wanted was a relationship with him, but it seemed as if I wasn't a priority.

It hurts like hell when a daughter doesn't have a relationship with her father. I think it's one of the worst things in the world. Without a father's love, a girl grows up insecure about her identity and womanhood. I felt unloved and unwanted. I couldn't understand why my dad didn't want to spend time with me like my friends' fathers did with them. Some of my friends' dads came to school to eat lunch with them. I'm sure that made them feel special. I can't ever remember a time when my dad came to eat lunch with me. Fathers who don't spend time with their daughters very well could cause them to waste their time looking for replacements in the wrong places.

Growing up, I spent many nights feeling vulnerable and unprotected. Vulnerable because my emotions were controlling me and causing me to make very poor decisions in my choices of men; unprotected because I didn't have very much guidance, leaving me to figure out men problems on my own. One of those problems was, "How to choose a good boyfriend."

As time went on and I began to date, I didn't know my father's absence would set the tone for my pattern of bad relationships. When I was a teenager, I vowed never to date a man similar to my dad. Most of the men I dated didn't appear to be like him on the outside but they sure had similar characteristics.

After being involved in bad relationships repeatedly, the fatherless daughter syndrome was brought to my attention through an article I read. According to Merriam-Webster's dictionary, syndrome is defined by a set of concurrent things (as emotions or actions) that usually form an identifiable pattern. The lack of a father/daughter relationship resulted in a pattern of failed relationships and repeated cycles of dysfunction in my life. This most important relationship became the model for the unhealthy relationships that I was involved in. As you can see, there's still a little girl inside every woman. The tests of her relationships will prove how damaged she is.

My dad gave me a poor example to follow to choose a man to be my mate. He was a liar, cheat, and woman beater. As a result, I found myself choosing men who are very similar. They are sweet and charming on the outside but literally beasts on the inside. I knew I deserved more but did not know how to make that mental transition. I was attracted to men who mirrored the neglected relationship that I had with my dad. I was not taught how to allow a man to pursue me, so I became the aggressor. My aggressive behavior materialized as clinginess that led to ruined relationships.

I really felt that I sabotaged some of my relationships because I lacked trust in myself and others. My communication skills were horrible. I had a difficult time verbalizing my feelings because of the pain in my soul. Whenever I tried to express my point of view with my partner about what I perceived to be a problem in the relationship, it came out in a very angry way. He would feel disrespected and I would feel unheard. Both of us would leave the conversation very frustrated. If later he tried talking to me about the issue, I would become defensive as I conjured up thoughts and overly sensitive feelings from past relationships. I wanted a close connection with my father but our unresolved issues separated us. As such, I think this led to my biggest problem with men which was I didn't understand them. I compared them to each other because the problems are similar. My issues drove me into isolation and suspicion. I was a lonely mess but didn't understand the depths of my pain. I was smiling on the outside but scarred on the inside.

Wanting so badly to be loved pushed me to keep trying until one day the balloon popped. After a terrible break-up with the man to whom I was engaged to marry, I decided I needed help. I sought a counselor to help get me out of this mess before I wreaked myself. I thought to myself, it's impossible for me to have experienced so many failed relationships and there not be anything wrong. I decided to stop blaming the men and instead look internally to find out what was wrong with me. I refused to go into another relationship with these unmet needs, unresolved issues, and unhealed hurts. Therefore, I took myself off the market. No more dating for me. I faced the thing I feared the most…loneliness. I wanted to be whole. I was tired of losing at the game of love. Sitting in the counselor's office I felt like a sick patient waiting to see the doctor. I filled out my intake sheet and attempted to answer all the questions about my past. As I was writing, I could remember something about my childhood that always bothered me. In my childhood, my dad gave me a lot of broken promises. As a result I didn't trust men easily. I put a lot of fences around my heart. Searching for ways to prove their unfaithfulness, I wore myself out.

If you can relate to anything that I have said in this chapter, you may be classified as a wounded woman. Don't be discouraged. We all have been here at some point in our lives. Some are like me and more extreme than others. I was a drama queen who was controlling, needy, argumentative, passive and aggressive, jealous and insecure.

Don't close the book yet because I'm going to show you how to walk in your healing. To successfully answer the question of this chapter's title, all one needs to do is acknowledge experiencing some of the signs and symptoms addressed in this chapter.

SIGNS OF A WOUNDED WOMAN

- **Anxiety**
- **Depression**
- **Anger**
- **Hurt**
- **Insecurity**
- **Neediness**
- **Emptiness**
- **Jealousy**
- **Fear**
- **Loneliness**
- **Misery**
- **Guilt**
- **Shame**

Write down all the ways you feel damaged by neglect or abuse by a father or a partner.

_____

_____

_____

_____

_____

Do you find it hard to trust others?

_____

_____

_____

_____

_____

_____

Are you normally critical of others?

_____

_____

_____

_____

_____

Is there a wound that repeats itself in your relationships?

_____

_____

_____

_____

_____

Chapter 3

THE WOMAN

A woman represents God's idea of showing off. She was an idea in His head but when she came into existence, she became a Wow factor. This may be the reason he named her Wo-man. You are special. You may not feel so special because of the things you have gone through… but you are. There has never been a creature made quite like us. You are originals.

1.Her Purpose

According to the Small Business magazine, the "Wow" factor is a term used to describe a company that goes above and beyond customer expectations in delivering a great product and service experience. When God created woman, He went above and beyond. I want to build this foundation before I start talking about the make-up of a woman. It is important to understand the why of a creation before talking about its what. God created woman for a purpose. Paul says, "Woman was made for man" (1 Cor. 11:9). This might explain why you have a very difficult time dealing with failures in your relationships. It was not man's idea to create woman but God's idea to create her for the man. It was arranged by God himself. Then God said, "It is not good that man should be alone; I will make him a helper fit for him" (Gen. 2:18-24). Listen to me single women, you are some man's wife but make sure it's the right fit. So now you know your purpose for being created. Please don't get me wrong. This is not your only purpose in life but it's your purpose for being created.

2. Her Make-Up Heart Emotions Skills

How did God make woman? The bible says He formed her out of the rib of the man and later brought her to him. If you were to parallel this scripture with how modern day wives are formed, you would easily see that it takes far more time for the woman to be formed into being a wife than God's creation of her. It's not an overnight job. Being a good wife requires some molding.

If the man of your dreams has not shown up, the reason may be that you are not ready for him. When you are ready, he usually appears. Counterfeits come on a daily basis so you have to be a woman of discernment to know the difference. It is very easy to start making permanent decisions on temporary feelings. This is yet another reason why women get wounded. A lack of patience can cause you to miss out on your promise. Patience is not something practiced every day. It is actually one of the hardest things for women to exercise. Most single women lack the patience needed to become fit helpers for their husbands. I am guilty. There have been times in my life when I have tried to help God out, only to have the situations end in disaster. I learned that the key is to trust God even when His steps can't be traced. God knows us better than we know ourselves.

For the LORD God is a sun and shield; the LORD will give grace and glory; No good thing will he withhold from them that walk uprightly.
(Psalm 84:11 KJV)

God made woman from man's rib to be the protector of his heart. Scientifically, the rib cage protects the lungs and heart. Without the rib cage, those organs would be exposed to life threatening injuries. Because they were created to be the protectors of men's hearts, women usually see things concerning their mates before they happen. God gave women built-in radars to detect trouble. He shows them how to pray for their future husbands even before they meet them. A wise woman knows how to watch and pray and protect her mate from danger. It's hard to believe but is very true. When you are sensitive to the Holy Spirit, He will wake you up with things to pray about for your future husband. During this time of prayer, God will also reveal your husband's strengths as well as weaknesses. You, being the woman fit for him, must learn how to be spiritually alert.

Your Heart

While single, it is important to guard your own heart from contamination. If you master this in singlehood, you will be well equipped to transfer it into your marriage. A similar concept but slightly different. Let's talk a little bit about guarding your heart.

Above all else, guard your heart for everything you do flows from it.
(Proverbs 4:23 NIV)

Guarding your heart requires being careful about what you allow to go into your thoughts. You have to be able to scan your thoughts before allowing them to have place in your mind. Every thought that comes to mind is not a good thought. It is your decision to determine whether you will allow that thought to drive your actions and behavior. How does this affect you as a single woman? I'm glad you asked. When you meet a guy for the first time and you think he's a good mate candidate, your mind usually goes into overdrive. You already have seen the wedding, honeymoon, and baby. Your emotions are all over the place. This is not good because your emotions can cause you to become anxious. Your body language comes across as desperate and needy. Your anxiety controls your speech and manipulates the relationship in another direction. Simply because you think he's a good mate candidate does not mean this connection will become a romantic relationship. Eligible single men will come into your life for reasons other than being your husband. Some relationships with the opposite sex were created just to be kingdom friendships. You must be willing to ask God for wisdom to distinguish the reason. I have met a few nice eligible single men on my journey. Unfortunately, after seeking God about each situation, I realized they were to be my friends, not my husbands. They were husband material, just not mine. It can be a hard pill to swallow. It feels like waiting in a long line only to get to the front and be told by the receptionist, "I'm sorry, you're in the wrong line for marriage." How frustrating to have to start over again when you thought you were there. Guarding your heart can prevent major disappointments. It takes a secure woman to accept the fact that an eligible single man is not her husband.

Secondly, guarding your heart means avoiding self-deception. I have seen countless single women deceive themselves into thinking that certain men were destined to be their husbands. Some of the men they believed to be their husbands never even asked them out on a date. I have been there before. Earlier in my walk with the Lord, my mind tricked me into thinking a certain single but engaged man was my husband and that he was about to marry the wrong girl. I was very young in the Lord and extremely naïve. It was a mess. The gentleman ended up marrying the girl and they are still happily married until this day. Can this happen to women? Yes, all day long. I have seen it happen so many times until it's ridiculous. Furthermore, there are women who believe their local married pastor should be married to them. They pray against the current marriage and wreak havoc on the relationship. This is confusion. It's not even biblical. Guard your heart. Don't allow self-deception to speak louder than common sense.

Your Emotions

Women are very emotional beings. They depend on their emotions to give them signs for making decisions. Being that they are emotional, it's important for them to surround themselves with accountability partners, be they single or married. Accountability partners will not tell them what they want to hear. Rather, they will be honest with them, even if it hurts. Don't be afraid to bounce things off of those who are married. They will normally give sound advice. Deciding to establish a relationship with an incompatible person because of loneliness happens every day. I have heard the saying, "It is better to wait than to wish that you had!" If I had a dollar for every time I heard that I would be rich. Don't allow your emotions to control your life. Doing so can be costly. If you are just feeling like you need a fix, go shopping, to the spa or salon.

Your Skills

The heart of her husband doth safely trust in her…she will do him good and not evil all the days of her life.

(Proverbs 31:11-12 NIV)

Another translation reads, her husband puts his confidence in her, and he will never be poor. Are you the type of woman a man can trust with his livelihood? If he had a million dollar business, could he depend on you to increase or decrease his wealth? This Proverbs 31 woman was industrious. She brought assets to the relationship. A good man is looking for a woman who is an asset, not a liability.

Protecting his heart, as his wife would, gives him confidence in you. Part of guarding his heart is allowing him to feel safe around you. Can he trust that you have his back? Are you with him for the long-haul? Men really want to know this. They don't like feeling like an opportunity. As a woman, you don't want to be involved with a guy who thinks you are just a playmate for now, and all the while he's looking for someone "better" to come along. There are men who are opportunist. As long as the relationship benefits them, they will remain. But the moment they find someone who can take them higher financially, they will dismiss you. Women, please beware during your singlehood as there are men out there who fit this description. Just don't allow yourself to get caught up in this type of relationship. The hurt that you would experience -- thinking that you have someone who truly loves you when, in reality, they sought you out because of what you could do for them -- would be unbearable.

All of God's creation was good. You are neither a defect nor a mistake. You have been chosen by God to fulfill His destiny for your life. Don't allow past mistakes to rob you of your womanhood. A woman is precious. She is made to be adored. A good man will recognize his pearl when he sees it. Too many women are trying to get the wrong people to see their value. Fortunately, those people are blinded to your assets. Don't try to convince them of your worth.

How do you see yourself as a woman?

_____
_____
_____
_____
_____

What purpose has God given you in His Kingdom?

_____
_____
_____
_____
_____

What are some ways you can guard you heart?

_____
_____
_____
_____
_____
_____

Are you prepared to be a helper fit for him (future husband)?

_____
_____
_____
_____
_____
_____

Chapter 4

Rejection: The Root Cause

Chapter 2 includes a lot of information about some of the symptoms and unhealthy patterns of being wounded. After revisiting many events in my life, I discovered that rejection by my father was the root cause of my pain. Listen to me closely and you might identify with some of these issues as a result of rejection. One night while I was going through the process of healing, I literally felt the pain of my soul. My soul was hurting as if it had sores inside of it. I felt like somebody had cut me with a knife and gutted me. I began to grieve and cry but still no relief. I now realized that God wanted me to feel and identify with this pain of rejection that had followed me all of my life. It was like a ghost; it would show up every time I felt like I was not being accepted.

In relationships, guys give mixed signals. Please accept them as warning signs to prevent heart break. Men said things to me like "I love you with all of my heart!" but their actions were far from it. Being the insecure woman that I was from previous unhealthy relationships, I became confused. I was that person who took things at face-value. I figured if they didn't mean it, then they wouldn't say it. As common courtesy, I tried to give everyone the benefit of the doubt. However, that was not the right decision in the relationships. The more I believed in and tried to affirm those empty words, the more distant they became. I began to think I was doing something terribly wrong. I couldn't understand how an attractive, intelligent, and a kind woman such as I was forced to face rejection.

The next time I paid closer attention because I was ready to truly get to the bottom of this thing so that I could be totally free. During my prayer time, the Holy Spirit revealed that I had a silent cry for acceptance and a deep craving for closeness in my relationships. He reminded me, that I would go to the deepest ends to find the love I longed for. Unfortunately, I didn't receive the closeness I desired because the people from whom I was trying to get it were unable to give it to me because they were emotionally bankrupt. I was too emotionally injured and subconsciously repeated old habits. I thanked God for the revelation but wondered what I should do when I got to this point. While most people would ignore the rejection or look for ways to numb the pain with drugs, alcohol, casual sex, work, or an alternative lifestyle, I found the pain too big to be ignored. In order to get rid of it, I had to deal with it or it would deal with me.

Let's take a look at the definition of rejection: to refuse to accept, submit to, believe, or make use of; to turn down. I dealt with all these in my childhood when my father was too busy to develop a relationship with me. This ghost of rejection haunted me for years. I didn't understand it at the time; I just thought I had serious cases of bad luck.

What were some of the manifestations of rejection in my relationships? The list could be monumental so I'll only share a few of them. At the top of my list were feeling unwanted, used, and unloved, followed closely by crushed self-esteem because of my perceived disapproval. It's easy to feel rejected when a man doesn't call you back after a date that you thought went so well. Or how about when you've spent years in a relationship and your partner marries another woman instead of you. The pain from the latter hurts so deeply that it was difficult for me to recover. Bitterness erupted. Many women can

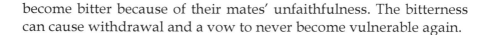

become bitter because of their mates' unfaithfulness. The bitterness can cause withdrawal and a vow to never become vulnerable again.

After too many blows of rejection to the heart, self-rejection can become prevalent. Women who struggle with self-rejection have come to the conclusion that they are worthless. Since others have rejected them, they unconsciously reject themselves. This can often lead to self-hatred. The damage from self-hatred is just as serious as rejection from others.

What causes rejection? The reasons are numerous. Misunderstanding someone's intent is a very common one. Another is trying to keep at bay those persons who should not be allowed into your life. And then there is envy. There are men who pursue women of a certain status to feed their egos. However, once in a relationship, they have to contend with a "lifestyle" that makes them think the women are above their caliber. Instead of communicating their concerns, they handle the women in very disrespectful ways.

I believe rejection is the root that causes wounds in women's lives. It produces all the other unhealthy branches, i.e., bitterness, anger, addiction, resentment, feeling of abandonment, loneliness, depression, to name a few. Unhealthy trees are that way because the roots are unhealthy and must be destroyed. I know you have to be tired of hurting. Trying to find someone to validate you is a defeated journey going nowhere. Allow God to destroy the root of rejection and supplant it with His healing.

During my time of evaluation, I realized everything happens for a reason. I may not have understood the reason but I trusted that things were working in my favor. I was not sure what in the world was wrong but I knew that I just had to allow this pain to pass through me. I wished that I could pull it up and out and never feel it again but it was not that simple. What was I doing wrong? As I was riding down the highway, God answered my question. He said my oil filter needed replacing and my oil needed to be changed. I started to visualize that in the natural as it relates to an automobile and recalled the importance of changing the oil. When your oil is not changed routinely, it will cause your engine to malfunction and your car to break down. The rejection in my soul had been a lot like the dirty oil in a car. I had carried this pain for so long that it had starting to wear me down emotionally, physically and spiritually to the degree that I was underperforming in other areas of my life. I needed intervention badly…my soul hurts were destroying my happiness. I experienced a trigger on this day and reflected on a very trying time in one of my relationships. My soul was literally hurting like a fire was lit to it. I could feel the cuts inside. I cried out to God for total healing. I thought I was healed from the majority of this pain but evidently there was still a root that had not been pulled up. Here I was again encountering rejection after all the years I had refrained from dating. Sad to say, but nothing had changed. Ladies, it doesn't matter how awesome you look on the outside or how much money you have in your bank account, you still can be a wounded, nice-looking intelligent woman with issues. You would think a man would want a woman who seemingly has it all together, but news flash! Those women get rejected, too.

The effects of rejection lead women to try to find relief, their value, and self-worth. During an episode of feeling this pain, you just want it to be over. You wish that you could take a bottle of medicine, fall asleep and awake totally healed. Most of the time you search for relief to deaden the pain in different ways. For me, I became a workaholic to drown out the intense sound of my pain, but that didn't work. I just became a tired wounded woman.

The answer for dealing with rejection cannot be found in external vessels. It's definitely an inside job. You have to stop seeking acceptance from everyone else and allow the Holy Spirit to heal you from the inside out. He is your first approval. He believes in your worth. *"Accept one another, then, just as Christ accepted you in order to bring praise to God."* (Romans 15:7) Christ accepted you so you should accept yourself. If others have rejected you, so what, it's their loss. Keep it moving and don't be discouraged by other people's actions.

After reading this chapter, have you identified the root cause of your pain?

_____
_____
_____
_____
_____

What are your top three relationship pattern mistakes?

_____
_____
_____
_____
_____
_____
_____

How do you respond to rejection? Do you fall apart? Try to convince others to accept you? Do you shut down? Or do you walk away?

_____

_____

_____

_____

_____

_____

_____

Chapter 5

Overcoming Rejection

Rejection is a type of communication. It sends a message that says you are unsatisfactory to someone else. To reject someone means to despise, refuse, avoid or turn away from. The message has a way of making the recipient feel unwanted, unaccepted, and unloved.

Here are several examples of incidents that could happen in relationships where the message is sent via verbal or non-verbal communication. Your mate is feeling smothered, but rather than communicate this to you orally, he starts to withdraw from the relationship. His non-verbal actions can be translated as rejection that later produces hurt and anger. Another example is he tells you he's going to call you at a certain time that day, but doesn't. As a matter of fact, you don't hear from him for several days. Even then, he doesn't bother to explain why he didn't call when he said he would. His verbal actions still leave you feeling offended and upset. You were angry and wondering what went wrong. You stalked him on his social media sites, questioned his friends, threw temper-tantrums, and the whole nine yards to try to make sense of the situation. He, on the other hand, didn't feel like he had done anything wrong. He's accustomed to not doing what he promised. While you were losing sleep, he was doing just fine.

How can you overcome the emotions felt when you receive these type messages? First, realize that the person's value system may differ from yours. Second, they may be wounded, just not in the same areas as you. Next, what may be important to you may not be that important to them. Lastly, if the same message is repeated, it is important to address how you feel with them. If they care about your personal feelings, they will change.

When single women expect more out of the relationship than men are ready to give, they set themselves up for disappointment that can lead to feeling rejected. This famous saying speaks volumes: *Men play at love to get sex while women play at sex to get love.* Women equate sex to commitment. It is so important to define the relationship early.

The way messages are received has a lot to do with overcoming rejection. Have you ever been in a room with a friend listening to a speaker only to later discover that two completely different messages were heard? People receive messages based on their perceptions and experiences. The speaker said, "In order to change your life one must be willing to change their thought processes." You heard paradigm shift but your friend, who normally internalizes rejection, heard something different. She felt as if the speaker was personally attacking her character. She's normally on the defensive end so instead of hearing that message through the eyes of empowerment, she received it as something negative.

Overcoming rejection requires cleaning your filters. The filters represent your core beliefs. Your beliefs represent your thought life. Your thought life affects your behaviors. When you change what you believe about yourself, your perception of YOU will also change. If you believe that you are a valuable person, no one can make you devalue yourself. Rejection then becomes something that rolls off of your back because you are secure in YOU.

Another solution to overcoming rejection is **upgrading your value system**. It is important to see yourself through the eyes of God instead of man. Men use rejection as a means of manipulation to control women. If your value system is not strong, you can easily be manipulated. I have had men reject me because I didn't conform to their way of doing things or when I held them to a certain standard. They would discount my good ideas or not even ask for them. Their actions were designed to make me become a "yes" man. If I didn't comply with their demands, I was immediately ostracized. Communication would be limited until I backed off and allowed them to do what they wanted. Be careful when this happens because it signifies that the relationship is one-sided. Don't get caught up in thinking you cannot live without him. In a healthy relationship, you and your mate must be willing to agree to disagree. Anything different from compromise is manipulation and control.

Once you clean your filters and upgrade your value system, you start to understand that God's plans for you are greater than what you have been experiencing. You begin to realize how special your life is and that you don't have to settle for less than God's best. Gaining victory in this area of your life will be very helpful in future relationships. Don't be afraid to identify and examine what makes you feel rejected. When you identify the feelings, replace them with the truth of God's word. Don't allow rejection to speak louder than the truth. God's word tells us that you are accepted into his family.

For he chose us in him before the creation of the world to be holy and blameless in his sight. In love he predestined us for adoption to son-ship through Jesus Christ, in accordance with his pleasure and will – to the praise of his glorious grace, which he has freely given us in the One he loves.
(Ephesians 1:4-6 NIV)

The opposite of rejection is acceptance. When men refuse to accept you, God chooses you. Before the foundations of the world, He knew the plans for your existence.

Overcoming rejection will remove the pain and enable you to move on to a life with no regrets. When you truly become healed from the fear of rejection, you can live the life of your dreams. Rejection holds you back in a mold. It is a very superficial way to live. Break the mold and become fearless. You must be willing to avoid seeking the approval of men and accept God's unconditional love toward you. In Galatians 1:10, Paul says it best:

Am I now trying to win the approval of human beings, or of God? Or am I trying to please people? If I were still trying to please people, I would not be a servant of Christ.

You cannot serve two masters. You will either love the one or the other. It is impossible to be faithful to both. Remember the only word that counts is the Holy Bible. Robert S. McGee, author and president of Search Resources, says:

You can ultimately seek either the approval of men or the approval of God as the basis of our self-worth. You cannot seek both. God wants to be the Lord of our lives, and He is unwilling to share that rightful lordship with anyone else. Therefore, the only way you can overcome the fear of rejection is to value the constant approval of God over the conditional approval of people.

There's a quote from Alice Hunt that truly inspired me. She said, "Rejection is God's Protection." I believe this now more than ever. There were men in my life who I thought I needed but later realized

I was better off without them. You usually attract the type of men men who mirror your emotional state at the time. If your self-esteem is low, you likely will choose a partner who struggles with the same issue. If you're broken in spirit because of a previous relationship, many times the man that you gravitate to is dealing with the same thing. Have you ever witnessed two divorced people connecting through their pain? It's like a magnet. They are of like minds and hearts and are drawn to each other. But once the pain subsides, they discover they have nothing in common. If you desire better for your relationship, you have to become better.

What are some of the unmet needs, unhealed hurts and unre-solved issues that you have experienced in your relationships?

_____

_____

_____

_____

_____

How can you overcome the emotional damage from your past?

_____

_____

_____

_____

_____

_____

_____

Now that you have identified some negative emotions, how can you replace them with the truth of God's word?

_____

_____

What type men have you been attracting?

_____

_____

_____

_____

_____

Chapter 6

UNPACK THE PAIN

Pain can be defined as that emotion in your life that you have not dealt with. For example, the pain you feel when you have been cheated on more than once can create a wall around your heart that locks others out and you in. Your way of dealing with the pain, falsely, I might add, is to lock yourself in. But have you considered that what you actually were doing was locking in the pain that would only allow you to enter into what was a semblance of a relationship in the future. Your heart really would not be in it. What would be the outcome? Your love interest would get fed up with not being able to reach you emotionally and opt out of the situation. The locked in heart can hinder your growth personally as well as relationally. You know it's there and you continue nurturing it so that it cannot heal. Now is the time to ask God to show you any and every thing that hinders you from giving and receiving true love. Tell him you want to be made whole.

What happens if you continue to ignore the wounds that cause the pains? Emotional wounds, if not dealt with, remain silent and latent until awakened in you or against others whom you are in relationship with. Pain will not magically disappear either. It will stifle your growth and development spiritually, personally, and professionally. You will feel like a prisoner of pain with a life sentence. A lot like the children of Israel who wandered in the wilderness because of their disobedience and unbelief. Unbelief is a tricky thing because if you don't believe that you have a problem then you can never solve it.

As Sun Tzu, traditionally credited as the author of The Art of War, an extremely influential ancient Chinese book on military strategy, stated thousands of years ago, in order to defeat your enemy, you must know your enemy. You have learned about some of your "enemies," the signs, symptoms, and root causes of your wounds. In Chapter 2, we spoke about how being neglected as a child produced long-term wounds. Overwhelming neglect in childhood or adulthood can make you vulnerable. The need to be wanted clouds your good judgment and forces you to settle into a relationship that is not optimum for you. It's like going into battle without your weapons. When a woman feels neglected in any area, she seeks solace for that pain anywhere she can find it. The struggle for her is filling the internal void but not with an external force. She has to come to grips with the fact that she can only be healed by the Creator filling the void and, sometimes, months of counseling.

If you've ever pulled a scab off of a sore, you know how ugly it looks and how badly it hurts. Equally as ugly and painful is peeling the layers off of your broken heart. In both situations, the peeling is necessary for healing to begin. Think about all the relationships you've had and why they ended badly. How did you respond to the hurt? Regardless of who was at fault, did you unpack the pain?

The Samaritan woman in John 4:7-18 is a prime example of a wounded woman who neglected to unpack her pain. According to v18, she had five unsuccessful relationships and was involved in another. Searching to find someone who would give her the love and attention she sought, she ended up bankrupt every time. Luckily, she ran into a Man who was able to meet her physical, emotional, and spiritual needs. He began to ask her questions that required her to think about the direction she had taken in her relationships for far too long.

The life of the Samaritan woman is the life of most wounded women waiting on Mr. Right. Like the Samaritan woman, they fail to check the inner hurt that causes the repeated cycle. Like the Samaritan woman, the relationships that you entered into were not healthy from the outset because you had not unpacked the pain. Recognize the unhealthy patterns that brought you into the relationship in the first place and commit to unpacking the pain.

Let's look at some of the "wounds" you need to unpack. **You cannot cultivate strong relationships when your inner core is not solid.** You must focus on rebuilding the inner person so that the outside shines. I have felt neglected in some relationships but didn't realize this feeling was planted in me during my childhood and, over the years, grew many unhealthy branches from that strong root. I became very resentful toward my partners because I felt it was their responsibility to make me happy. This is too much of a burden to put on anyone. Happiness and nurturing begins with you. It is a tough pill to swallow, but yet it's the honest truth.

Another wound that needs unpacking is jealousy, which will require you to define why you are jealous. Jealousy is normally rooted in fear. People fear something being taken away from them. What God has for you is for you. No one can take away what belongs to you. If it leaves, then that just means it wasn't yours to begin with. You may have wanted it to be but God knows best what you need. This is when you have to put your confidence in God and not yourself.

What about insecurity? People become insecure because they don't see the value within themselves. When you understand your worth, you will not feel compelled to get others to see that you are important. Knowing how valuable you are as a person can give you confidence in your potential. Thinking lowly of one's self produces a spirit of fear. One way to keep your head above insecurities is to know what God says to and about you. *For God hath not given us the spirit of fear; but of power, and of love, and of a sound mind.* (2 Tim. 1:7 KJV)

Unpacking the fear of abandonment will increase your trust bank and decrease your need to control. The pain from not being able to control another is probably the worst. It takes too much energy trying to get an adult to do what you want them to do. I have tried to control my relationships by being around my mate 24/7. I felt if we were together all the time, nothing would destroy our bond. Technically, it wasn't about us being together that was important to me but being able to monitor his every move. I quickly learned that I was not responsible for nor could I control another person's actions. I was only responsible for mine. If a relationship is strong, it will stand the tests of time. If he loves you and only you, he will not want to jeopardize the relationship. Ladies, you have to allow men to come to this conclusion on their own. Being extra nice and super supportive will not help if his character is that of an unfaithful man. Give them the benefit of the doubt. Let them go and stop trying to control them. They are not your property, but God's property.

Pay attention to your emotions. Unpacking depression and anger will bring joy to your soul. Keep a log of the times when you seem to get depressed – i.e., when you feel very sad, hopeless, unimportant, guilty, or lose interest or pleasure – or become angry. Notice what is running through your mind when the depression hits. For me, depression usually came during times when I felt I was not in control of my personal life. Arrest the thought and then replace the negative emotion with a positive. If you allow depression to linger, it will get

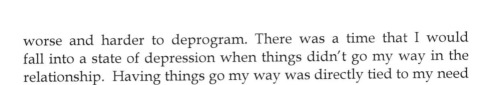
worse and harder to deprogram. There was a time that I would fall into a state of depression when things didn't go my way in the relationship. Having things go my way was directly tied to my need to control. Then anger set in.

Suppose you are still angry about the last break up and desperately want to move forward. You probably are asking yourself, "How do I unpack the anger that I am feeling as a result of what I have gone through in past relationships?" My answer to you is, acknowledge that the damage is done but that you will not allow anyone to rob you of your present happiness. Continuing to hold on to the anger will not change the outcome but it could create a health problem for you. Unhealed anger will steer you toward a person of like feelings and away from any potentially good relationships in the future.

Additionally, being angry is a big part of your unhappiness. You need to find out what's triggering the anger. I usually became angry in my relationships when my mates told me that they were going to do something but they never did what they said they would do. My response was to lash out with criticism. (Subconsciously, this anger stemmed from the disappointment I experienced in my childhood.) It's best to stop anger in its tracks before it destroys you and the persons involved. Identify what triggers your anger so that you can be free from all these negative emotions that hinder your healthy state of mind. These painful wounds have taken control of your physical and mental state of mind, and it's time to get back everything the enemy has stolen from you. You may have other triggers. You can get rid of them all the same way, by unpacking the pain.

Now that you have been enlightened, you can begin to unpack the pain. Keep reading, please. To drive home the importance of dealing with the root causes of wounds and pain, I want you to write down five emotional pains that you deal with often. Things such as rejection, abandonment, anger, jealousy, etc., come to mind. Please be as honest as possible. After you've finished, take some time to look at what you have written. Take into consideration what triggers some of these emotions. Call someone you trust and ask them to list five emotions they believe you have struggled with. Match their responses to your answers and see if they are closely related. Accept the good things and embrace the bad.

Write down five painful emotional challenges?

_____
_____
_____
_____
_____

Write down five painful emotional challenges from a friend's perspective?

_____
_____
_____
_____
_____
_____

If you continue to ignore or deny the pain, will it magically disappear? Why not?

_____

_____

_____

_____

_____

_____

_____

Can you see romantic relationships improving with the current emotional baggage that you are carrying?

_____

_____

_____

_____

_____

_____

Chapter 7

DEPROGRAM AND REPROGRAM

Is it possible to become a prisoner to your pain? Absolutely! Pain can put you in a cell. At some point you must realize being locked away is harmful. If you continue to live life as if nothing is wrong then your denial becomes your prison. It's a lot like being overweight. A person is aware that they're overweight and need to lose weight but they are in denial about being able to deal with the process of losing weight. Therefore, they remain in that position rather than deprogramming and reprogramming their minds to lose the weight. Wow! This is you in your wounded state until the cell door of your mind swings wide open and you decide enough is enough. It's at this point that you want to be free from the prison of your past. When this happens, a light of hope comes on and you realize there's a better way.

In order to move into healthy ways of thinking, the old computer chip that was running in your mind must be wiped clean and reprogrammed. Realize that you are made in the image of God and everything God made was good. You are God's masterpiece. Despite the wounds and pains you suffered in life, they cannot compare to God's original plan for your creation. Please say this to yourself, "I am fearfully and wonderfully made by God. I am his handiwork created in His glory. I am the apple of His eye and have been approved by the Most High, Jesus Christ.

Just because others wronged you doesn't mean they did so because you were a bad person. You were a good person with bad baggage. Speak God's word over your life and positive affirmations. Look for healing quotes that pertain to your particular brokenness. You will still feel the pain but now you are reversing those negative thoughts that once had control over your mind and emotions. Every day read a scripture from God's word that pertains to who you are in Christ. Next read a positive quote that pertains to healing your broken heart. After 30 days of deprograming and then reprogramming the mind, you will start to feel better. During this time you should not be distracted by dating. This is your time for inner healing so that you can be prepared for the right man when he comes your way.

A part of the reprogramming is spending time getting to know yourself so that you can love the little girl back to maturity. I want to first address the childhood pain that has followed you into adulthood. It is important to understand that your past cannot be changed. What happened in your dysfunctional families just that -- in your past. At this point the only thing you can change is how you respond to the pain from your past. I want you to literally go back and get that little girl that was neglected and abused physically or emotionally. Grab her from the place of her trauma and let her know everything is all right now. Tell her she has been placed in the hands of God and He will lead her out of the cave.

Put your arms around yourself and embrace the little hurting girl inside. Tell her you will take care of her from this point on. Let her know that you will guard her heart and help her make wiser decisions from this point on. As you do this, the memories of your past will start to surface but don't hold back the tears. Let them flow because this is the last time the pain is going to drive you into bad relationships. While the tears are flowing, your heart is finally grieving the loss of the things you desired but did not receive. Grieving is a part of your healing process. It is necessary to grieve so that you can release all of the negative emotions that have dictated your emotional responses up until now.

A reprogrammed mind will tell you to love yourself just as God loves you. People treat you the way you treat yourself. It is contagious. Spend time nurturing yourself by attending to your most important needs. Every human being has a need to be loved and enjoy social activities. Make an effort to do something you like at least once a month. As you unpack the pain and deprogram the old mind, you will begin to realize that you have neglected yourself the same way others have neglected you. Don't hold on to past pain. Every now and then, it's good to treat yourself. Go out and enjoy your favorite ice cream. If you like flowers, buy a bouquet of them. Why wait for someone else to give you what you can give yourself?

Get back to spending time grooming yourself with such things as skin massages, visits to the hair salon and nail shop. Empower yourself with knowledge to help you achieve your financial and career goals. These are examples of putting yourself on the front burner and not on the back burner. You are your greatest investment. If you don't take care of yourself, you will not be healthy enough to take care of others.

Write down where you believe the pain started?

_____
_____
_____
_____
_____
_____

What incidents trigger your emotional pain?

_____
_____
_____
_____
_____
_____
_____
_____

Write down five things that make you feel loved?

_____
_____
_____
_____
_____
_____

Chapter 8

FORGIVENESS

Unpacking the pain and seeking forgiveness are steps in the right direction to successfully meeting the man of your dreams. After you have unpacked the pain, you need to forgive yourself and others and ask God for His forgiveness, too. When things seem unfair in your life, you feel the need to find someone to blame. If you can't blame others, you blame God. And if you can't blame God, then you blame yourself. Become brave enough to let go of the offenses, broken promises, disappointments and what could have been. Let them go! Holding on to un-forgiveness robs you of pending joy. You have to be willing to stop pointing fingers and let the dead bury the dead.

Forgiveness is an action that seems uncommon in our culture because most people think if they forgive they have to forget. According to Merriam-Webster, forgiveness means to stop feeling anger toward (someone who has done something wrong); to stop blaming (someone); to stop feeling anger about (something). The definition is easier to read than practice. Depending on how deep the pain, your anger toward the person will not go away immediately but your decision to forgive puts your mind in position to become less angry. As time goes by, the anger will subside and sometimes it turns into mercy.

Why should you forgive your partner for causing you pain? When you forgive them for hurting you, you are actually healing yourself.

Harboring un-forgiveness toward your partner leads you to bitterness. This harms only you, not the person who inflicted the pain. Furthermore, while you're still bitter, they've moved on with their lives and forgotten about the entire incident. You, on the other hand, remember the incident like it was yesterday. This is too much control to give someone who has exited your life. By not forgiving them, you are allowing them to continue hurting you. Resolve the internal struggle before it destroys your peace of mind.

By forgiving, you are giving God the opportunity to work on your behalf. The scripture says, "Do not take revenge my dear friends, but leave room for God's wrath, for it is written: "It is mine to avenge; I will repay," says the Lord." (Romans 12:19, NIV). Jesus gives you the secret to winning wars. Most people don't understand the value in taking God at His Word. If you repay people for the harm done to you; it's revenge. But if you step out of the way and allow God to avenge you, He will complete a great work. This is your opportunity to humble yourself under the mighty hand of God.

Forgiveness also gives you the ability to move on with your life. A part of moving on is doing new things. Explore new hobbies. Take a sewing class, ballroom dancing or scuba diving. Cultivate new friendships. Refusing to forgive will keep you trapped in the pain. Not forgiving is more dangerous than letting it go. In addition to causing bitterness, it brings about resentment and health problems. It has a way of keeping you stuck in your past. You will remain tied to the person who hurt you. Even worse, you keep your negative emotions alive. You don't need to carry that load forever.

People have asked how to forgive a person who has caused so much pain. The best way to do this is by learning and choosing to forgive. Forgiveness is not a feeling, but a choice. Take your mind off the person(s) who inflicted you. Remember, just because you forgive doesn't mean you have to continue in the relationship. Commit the situation to prayer. Pray that the Lord will deliver you from the negative memories that have clogged your spiritual arteries. As you are praying, the Lord will give you grace to take the necessary steps to forgiveness. As He orders your steps, He will soften your heart. Allow the Holy Spirit to show you the hidden things in this situation. He will give you a new understanding that will help bring closure to the pain.

One of the ways you know you have forgiven is you stop trying to seek revenge. Another sign of forgiveness is when you see the person and the pain doesn't hurt as badly. Forgiveness is a work in progress and any small steps toward the decision should be celebrated. Forgiveness is proof that you are ready to move on to the next chapter in your life. Moving forward will give you the assurance that things are changing for the better.

Forgive the person or persons who caused the damage – you or your mate. Forgiveness is a sign of healing, recovering, and unpacking the pain. If the other person caused the pain, then it is up to you to take back your life. A part of taking back your life is accepting what happened. Remember, you attract men whose emotional states mirror yours at that time. Immediately move on; don't wallow in self-pity. It may take many months or years to heal but unpack the negative, pinned up emotions of neglect to prevent this cycle of pain from recurring. Unpacking the pain and seeking forgiveness are steps in the right direction to successfully meeting the man of your dreams.

Why is forgiveness important?

_____
_____
_____
_____
_____
_____
_____
_____

What happens if I don't forgive?

_____
_____
_____
_____
_____
_____
_____

How do I forgive when I'm still hurting?

_____
_____
_____
_____
_____
_____

How can I tell if I've truly forgiven?

_____
_____
_____
_____
_____
_____
_____
_____

Chapter 9

BREAKING THE CYCLE

Unmet needs and unresolved issues usually are the reasons women rush into new relationships before they heal from the past one. Many women feel that they can recover from the pain by finding someone else. If the root cause of the pain is not properly dealt with, the cycle will be repeated. How do you heal from the pain? Firstly, accept the fact that your last bad relationship didn't work out. It's over and you should learn from the experience. Take responsibility for the role you played in the demised relationship. Realize you may have brought unresolved baggage from a previous relationship or even from childhood into the mix. If a lot of the problems were coming from him, he has given you the opportunity to see what you don't want in a relationship. You now are empowered to know what characteristics will not fit in your love equation.

You can never do the same things and expect to get different results. You must always try to change in order to get change in your life. *The definition of insanity is doing the same thing over and over and expecting different results.* It's very simple. If you want something different you must take a different route. A part of taking a different route is becoming aware of the signs along the way. **Don't ignore red flags or avoid the obvious when you enter into a relationship with a guy, no matter how great he looks.** These are warning indicators that something needs to be reviewed or questioned. If he doesn't return your calls, he's not that in to you. If he makes promises and doesn't keep them, you're not that important to him. If he only calls late at night, chances are you are an after-thought or he lives with someone else. If he's late all the time for your dates, he's disrespectful and doesn't care about your feelings. This is a big one. If you've never met his friends or family after six months of dating, he has no plans of making you a part of his life.

Is he demanding and controlling? Are there too many gaps in his story about his current situation? Does he talk or ask about sex too early in the relationship? Does he refuse to admit when he's wrong? Is the only time that you see him is when you make the plans? How does he deal with his problems? Does he have uncontrollable outbursts, overeating problems, drug dependencies, etc.? If the answer to these questions is, yes, you need to slow your roll. That's why it is important to know what you want upfront instead of settling for what you don't want. Communicate early and it will save you and him time and heartaches. Red Flags are signals you get in your mind that say, take heed. Something doesn't fit the resume; some behaviors are damaging to my beliefs. Don't ignore these signals; use them to make mature choices.

I know you might be thinking things would be different if you were to date someone of a different race, age bracket, or gender. That's not the answer. The answer to breaking this vicious cycle begins by taking a journey within and dealing with the person in the mirror. It is not an external solution but an internal resolution.

Let's talk about the woman in the mirror. Who are you? Do you think you deserve better? The answer to these two questions will help you understand why you have accepted such bad treatment for so long. Men usually give you indicators early in the relationship. You sometimes ignore them because you want the relationship so badly.

Who you are is a woman who has been created to be a beautiful butterfly. You are to be respected, loved, and cherished. Anything contrary to that treatment is less than God's best for your life. For example, I used to allow men to give me broken promises and never apologize for what they had done. It happened one day one time too many. I was scheduled to meet up with someone and they never called to say they would be late. Their excuse was that they got caught up. I was truly offended because it seemed that whatever they were doing at the time was more important than meeting up with me, and they knew that I would wait. Wow, how disrespectful. You teach people how to treat you by little things such as that incident. Realize that you are important enough to set boundaries in your life. Don't allow people to walk in and out of your life as they please. You are special and should be treated that way. If you are the apple of God's eye then you should be the apple of your partner's eye. Although society changes, it is your responsibility to regain your territory and set the standards for your personal relationships.

Jesus is the captain of your ship. Let Him lead you. You must guard your heart with all diligence because out of it flow the issues of life. Take notice of previous patterns that led to your failed relationships and be determined to overcome the victim's mentality that every relationship will end in heart break. Make a list of all the men you have had relationships with up until now and what attracted you to each one of them. What was good or bad about the relationship? Were there similarities between the previous relationships? Questions like these will help you to identify and confront your wounds and the resulting pains.

The pains of insecurity, low self-esteem, clinginess, jealousy and suspicion attract the wrong types of men. If you reflect back on the characteristics of some of the men in your life, you will discover that they, too, had signs of low self-esteem, jealousy and insecurity. Remember, you normally attract people whose weaknesses mirror yours. The only way to solve this problem is to allow yourself time to heal. You must be willing to endure the process in order to break the cycle. Get the emotional cancer out so that you can enjoy the life that you deserve.

During this season of your life, focus on yourself instead of others. Discover what makes you happy. Design a vision map just for you. Revisit your dreams and goals. Write down every detail so that you can track your accomplishments. Master being the best that you can be. Harness your gifts and sharpen your mind. The more you get into yourself, the less time you will have to worry about a relationship. This is what I call "The off the market period" so that you can heal.

What does it mean to be off the market? As a realtor, whenever one of my houses didn't sell within 60 days of being on the market, I had to revisit every aspect of the transaction to figure out why. Usually it was priced too high or didn't show well. Sometimes I would suggest to my client to either lower the price or take it off the market and make a couple of changes to the house and the listing. When it was taken off the market, it was no longer for sale. It now was being revamped. Sometimes, you will need to allow yourself to be revamped. Stop dating for a while so that you can rebuild. Give yourself time to strengthen your inner man and change your perspective. How you see yourself is how other people will see you. Rebuild your values and your whole world will change. How long should you be off the market? That's totally up to you.

Breaking an old cycle will cause to create a new one. Get involved with different activities. Visit new places. Meet different types of people. Build stronger bonds with family and friends. After a while, you will start to see the shift in your personal life and relations. Just because you are single doesn't mean you have to be lonely. You can enjoy a great single life by making the necessary adjustments.

Find your inner self by taking some personality tests. These tests will help you understand why you do some of the things that you do. They can be enlightening to the type of mate you need in your life to complement your personality. Take time to understand your love language. Gary Chapman, relationship counselor and director of Marriage and Family Life Consultants, Inc., has a book titled, "The Five Love Languages." His list includes the following:

1. Words of Affirmation
2. Gifts
3. Acts of Service
4. Quality Time
5. Physical Touch

These five love languages express heartfelt commitment to your mate.

Discovering your purpose is a big part to reclaiming your life. You know what the bible says about your purpose for being created. But who were you created to become? What's your goal in life other than getting married? Identify your unique talents and gifts. Understand what makes you tick. All women have something they are passionate about. When that is fulfilled, they feel like their mission on earth has been accomplished. Your partner cannot find this for you. You must be able to identify and recognize it before you become one with anyone else. It is your DNA. Your life purpose is what makes the person that you are. I've seen so many women get married trying to find their purpose only to end up empty and depressed. If you don't know who you are and what you you're created to become before you get married, it will be a struggle after marriage. Two whole people are a lot better than two halves.

How do I break the vicious cycle of disappointing relationships?

_____

_____

_____

_____

_____

_____

_____

_____

Chapter 10

HURRY UP AND WAIT

The phrase "Hurry up and wait" is a humorous one used to refer to a situation in which one is forced to hurry in order to complete a certain task, or arrive at a certain destination, by a specified time only for nothing to happen at that time, often because other required tasks are still awaiting completion. According to the Wikipedia Encyclopedia, the phrase may have originated in the United States military in the 1940s.

Single women are always in a hurry to marry, but God is not in a rush to manifest it. Many have asked, "What's taking God so long?" God is asking, "Why are you in such a hurry?" For many of you, your biological clock is ticking and you feel like you are getting older. You start to question whether you are called to be a Nun. After so many bad dates and broken relationships, it's easy to feel like you are walking down the wrong path. Let's look at the word hurry. Hurry means to do something quickly. You may want your food quickly or your hair finished fast but a marriage partner is not something you want thrown together.

Preparing for a lifetime mate is a task. Both parties involved need to be mature. Marriage is for mature people. It's not for the faint of heart but it is for those who understand the different dynamics to the covenant. A marriage covenant is an agreement and a vow one person makes with another. It is a vow that both parties make before God and man. Divorce is not an option. The marriage vows quote,

"Until death do us apart." How many people have repeated these very words but are no longer married? I am one of them. I got married because I was anxious. I had no idea what I was getting myself into. I thought everything was going to be smooth and manageable. I never thought things would get out of control the way that they did. After the seventh year, there was a major change and I didn't know what to do. I was miserable and felt like I was the only one that wanted the marriage. My ex-husband became bitter about several things and decided to live like a single man. His bitterness turned into hatred. He was so angry that he decided to leave our marriage bed and sleep on the couch.

Now that I'm out of the relationship, I realize these behaviors were attacks from the enemy. Unfortunately, I didn't have the proper tools to respond to the conflicts. I was operating off limited knowledge. There are marriage-destroying spirits. The first attack was to shut down our communication channels. The enemy knew if he could keep us from communicating then it wouldn't be long before we separated. We separated physically by sleeping in different rooms but our hearts separated spiritually long before then. We walked around the house like total strangers. My mind was constantly racing thinking about the things he could be doing while he refused to talk to me. When he got up in the morning, he wouldn't even say hello. It was terrible. We were behaving like kids. I tried to apologize but he wouldn't accept my apology. He didn't want counseling or anything. We were headed for big trouble and eventually divorced.

Marriage was designed by God and it will take the work of the Holy Spirit and two mature people to hold it together. When you marry outside of God's timing and His personal protocol, you set yourself up for failure. Here are a few common mistakes most singles make during their waiting period.

Seven Common Mistakes Single Women Make

1. Compromise

When you try to force marriage, you can miss important red flags. The counterfeits start to look real and you become easily deceived. If you have to lower your standards in order to be with him you are in a compromising condition. Anything worth having is worth waiting for.

2. Discontentment

Being unhappy with your current relationship status can cause you to become ungrateful about life all together. Great moments can be easily missed by concentrating on being married. Make the best of your NOW because tomorrow is not promised to anyone.

3. Impatience

Impatient can be defined as restlessness because of delay. Sarai was impatient about the promise and ended up with Ishmael before she got Isaac. Her decision not to wait caused so many problems that they continue even to today.

4. Loneliness

Long periods of singleness can be very lonely and miserable. Allowing the emotions of loneliness to dictate your decisions can be harmful. Allow loneliness to provide an opportunity for healing instead of making bad dating choices.

5. Jealousy

Don't allow other people who are getting married to make you become jealous because you are still single. Being single does not make you unfit. Be careful not to fall into the trap of rushing your time because you see others being connected to their spouses. Your time will come when you least expect it.

6. Validation

Many people want to be married because they think somehow they will feel better about themselves. Marriage does not validate who you are. Your validation and approval come from God. Please remember that it's better to wait than to wish that you had.

7. Sex Drive

Engaging in premarital sex is dangerous. It can cause you to feel an attachment to your partner faster than you should. Sex has a way of clouding your judgment and causing you to overlook the important stuff.

Be patient and don't skip steps. It means everything to the relationship. Your waiting period is not a holding pattern. It is a time of great reflection and growth. God is sovereign and He knows what He's doing in your life. His plans for you are good and not evil. He knows how much time and experience it will take in order for you to become the wife fit for the right mate. Please avoid rushing this most important process because it is definitely needed.

As I said earlier, when I got married, it was because I was tired of waiting and struggling financially. I was looking for a savior. I really thought I was ready because I had been celibate for some years and leading a singles ministry. I was definitely ready physically but not emotionally. The biggest problem I faced after being married was giving up my freedom. I was still single-minded and didn't adopt the principle of becoming one. I would go and come when I wanted without checking in. I was used to having freedom of choice and found it hard to adjust to my lifestyle change. I started having kids immediately and quickly graduated from being a parent of one to becoming a parent of four. My time management skills were already horrible but now I had to consider incorporating all the children into the equation. I was overwhelmed, frustrated, and depressed. I was happy to be married but didn't know that marriage would come with these many responsibilities. This is why I said, marriage is for mature people. It is not for the immature or impatient. It is definitely for those who have been processed.

What can you learn from my mistakes? Had I spent time during my waiting period learning better time management skills, how to become one in marriage, and how to respond to conflicts in marriage, I would have been prepared. I spent my waiting period complaining, discontent, lonely, and focusing on other people who were getting married. Can you see how I wasted my time? I don't want you to waste yours. Not only is it important to heal but it is also important to prepare. Please take full advantage of your singleness and let it prepare you for marriage. Our next chapter will focus on you becoming marriage material.

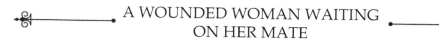

Why should I Hurry Up and Wait?

_____

_____

_____

_____

_____

_____

_____

_____

Chapter 11

MARRIAGE MATERIAL

Now that the wounds and pain cycles have been broken, you can discover the joy of giving and receiving true love in all your relationships.

I am here to tell you that love doesn't have to hurt. There are still more good men out there. You don't have to be lonely for the rest of your life. God has someone just for you. He wants you to be healed so that you can receive what He has been preparing for you all this time. Successful marriages can happen among two people who are willing to be interdependent and not co-dependent on each other. Research shows that 50 percent of marriages end in divorce. These are true facts but once a couple learns the tools of what it takes to have a successful marriage, it can work. Too often women approach marriage unprepared, unlearned, and with too much baggage causing the marriage to fail.

Many women want to be married but don't know what it takes to become marriage material. What are some of the qualities you need to become the woman he would love to marry? These are good thoughts that often are neglected during the early stages of a relationship. Let's face it, not all women are yet marriage material. There is still hope for those who are not if they are teachable.

Marriage is a lot like parenting. It doesn't come with instruction manuals. It requires a person to challenge themselves to learn the tools needed to be effective. In my opinion, one of the most important qualities to have is communication.

1. Communication

You must understand how to communicate with your mate in a way that is receptive. Men like kindness. My grandmother used to say, "You can kill a cat with kindness." I didn't understand what she meant at the time but 20 years later the light bulb came on. When you have an issue to discuss, please remember to be kind and not a nag. You will be heard much sooner with kindness than with repetitive nagging.

Becoming a good communicator requires a person to become a good listener. Be attentive and allow your mate to talk to you about anything. Understand that men use non-verbal language a lot especially when they don't feel like talking. This is not a personal attack against you; it's just how they are wired. Become comfortable with silence. Some men just want to feel your presence without holding a conversation. Another very critical component to communication is conflict resolution. Not knowing or embracing the art of conflict resolution has led to countless divorces. While you are single, learn how to manage stress, confront adversity, and express anger productively. All couples will, at times, come into conflict. Understanding how to seek solutions to your problems will resolve differences more quickly. A woman who is ready for marriage has to think before speaking. You cannot just say whatever comes to your mind. There will be times that you will need to step away from a heated situation and then address it at the appropriate time. I think all women can use some training in this area -- especially if you grew up in a household where anything goes. If your parents were accustomed to fighting physically and cursing verbally, your chances of repeating the same behaviors are great. In marriage there are a few things you should avoid. Never use physical or verbal abuse, call out names or say hurtful things such as, I don't love you. Knowing how to resolve conflicts with your spouse-to-be plays an important part in the success of your relationship.

2. Be Attractive

Men love attractive women. Attractive doesn't mean you have to be a super-model. It just means you care about your appearance. Spend time finding out about colors that complement your skin tone and body shape. There are image consultants who can help you find wardrobes that will complement your body type. Be sure to wear items that bring out the best in you. Every woman has the opportunity to look her best. Queens of all shapes and sizes: work your assets. Just a free tip, men love fashion but they don't get serious with a woman who is too seductive. Keep it classy/sassy. Love yourself by respecting your body and appearance. Practicing these habits before you're introduced to Mr. Right will make it much easier once you are together.

3. Self-Love

Self-love is the belief you hold that you are a valuable and worthy person. In order to truly love yourself, you must be able to accept your own strengths and weaknesses. Give yourself compassion. It's easy to become hard on you, but a part of loving you is to know when to lighten up and when to forgive. People who love themselves will take care of their basic needs such as eating properly, exercising, resting, and building healthy relationships. Knowing when to tell people no is most important to caring for you. Allowing people to walk all over you is self-destructive. A woman who is most attractive is one who loves herself.

4. Self-confident

Being self-confident is like a magnet that pulls men toward you. Men are drawn to women who are confident in themselves. This type of confidence usually comes when you have unpacked your pain and recognized your future. A woman who knows her purpose usually is very confident. This type of woman is focused and determined. She's also a God chaser. She's spent time with God so that He could give her courage and tenacity. God transforms anything that comes into contact with Him. I've seen prostitutes become deliverers and desperate women become determined. It is almost impossible to have spent time with God and remain the same. During your time of communing with Him, He reveals your purpose and treats you like a daughter. He taught me how to value myself because He values me. A confident woman knows what she is looking for and refuses to settle for less. Some women accept the first man who's willing to give them attention. Not so for confident women. They chose very wisely. God speaks into their spirit to empower them to think like Him. He exemplifies strength. That strength will translate to confidence and confidence is electrifying.

5. Respect

Women who are marriage material know how to respect their partners privately and publicly. Don't share his personal business with your girlfriends. This can be harmful to the relationship because when you decide to patch things up with him, your girlfriends still remember that you told them about his character and they can't seem to forgive him for his short-comings. Respect is shown in many ways. For some men respect is appreciation. For others, creating a homely atmosphere means the world to them. They seem to love when their wives are enthusiastic about taking care of the home. Making sure things are running smoothly around the home is a plus for many men. Most of the men I talk to about relationships are not picky. They just feel special when women are affirming them through nice gestures. Most men are not the entertaining type. They will depend on your nurturing spirit to entertain guests. If this is a weak area for you, please try to work on it while you are single.

6. Trustworthy

Be trustworthy, don't lie, sneak or betray him. Be honest, upfront, direct and loyal. If you make a commitment, please follow through with it. When it comes to relationship maintenance, trust, and consistency are key. A part of being trustworthy is to trust him. Give him space. Everyone needs time alone. Try not to snoop into his devices and personal social media sites. Respect his privacy. If there's something fishy going on, you will find out. What happens in the dark will come to the light. When healthy people feel safe, they will open up willingly.

7. Affection

Affection. Affection. Affection. I thought women loved affection but men love women who show affection. A part of showing affection can be physical or verbal. Let's start off with the supportive forms of being affectionate. Affirmation is everything to a man. Positive affirmation will make a man so much more secure and content in all areas of his life. If they don't receive it from their significant other they'll seek it elsewhere. Compliment him on the small things. Encourage him to succeed and he will pick up the world for you. Be attentive but not aggressive. Men like to feel wanted. When you make them somewhat of a priority on your list, good men will give you the shirt off of their backs in return. Physical affection includes things like holding hands, kissing them on the face, massages, etc. Whatever their love language, be prepared to cater to it without compromising your personal convictions.

8. Emotionally Stable

Emotional stability is a must. This entire book is about emotions and how destructive emotions can be in relationships. Follow some of the exercises in the previous chapters to become emotionally healed. Be adventurous, fun, and exciting with a sense of humor. Play sports with him. Be willing to do spontaneous things. What you are doing is creating moments that cannot be erased. In order for a man to see you as a necessary part of his life, you need to create the right kind of experiences that attract him emotionally. Don't force him to make a commitment, allow it to happen naturally. Fight the urge to talk about the relationship and spend time creating moments. Avoid being an emotional roller coaster. One day you're excited, the next you're depressed and the day after, he has become your enemy. Everyone is prone to having bad days and good days but when your emotions are unstable, you scare good men away. Emotionally stable people know how to keep their tempers under control.

9. Independence

A woman who is ready for marriage has graduated in many areas of her life. She knows how to run a household. How to balance her checkbook. She's somewhat financially stable and able to function on her own. A man likes to feel needed but not over-burdened. Everyone has experienced set-backs in life but if he has to take care of you like a child, it can be a burden. Being an independent woman will be an asset to his life and not a liability. Enhance the skills that he already has. In my opinion, a relationship is better when two can contribute to the goals of the marriage. Two whole people coming together spiritually, mentally, physically and financially are a masterpiece. Make sure you have a life of your own. He prefers having a partner and not a leech. Becoming financially independent is a big plus. If you are currently struggling in this area, spend time improving your credit and getting out of debt. Determine your strengths and weaknesses, then work to improve them both.

10. Sexual Companion

Last but not least, a marriage material woman knows how to love her man. She studies the male anatomy and spends time understanding what makes a man feel loved in bed. There are many books, articles and movies out there loaded with information. But if you are a godly woman, the Holy Spirit will give you some insight in this area as well. It is important to start praying for sexual compatibility while you are single. You will be amazed how things line up when you finally meet your mate. If you have had problems in this area please don't be afraid to reach out to a professional who can help. Sex is a very important part of marriage, so don't take it lightly. I have heard the many cries of married men relating to their sexual life. It can make or break a marriage. Some women who have experienced sexual abuse or had bad sexual experiences avoid having sex with their husbands. It is important to get to the root of this issue while you are single.

Your husband will be understanding and will grieve with you but he is expecting to bond with you through sex. Please don't deprive him of this very important part of your love life. I went through some healing as it pertains to sex. I have always thought it was dirty because of the things I experienced in childhood. I enjoyed it but never really saw it as important when I was married. It became a regimen after many years. This is a big mistake. Women, you must bring passion into your bedrooms. Affirm your husband so that he doesn't need Delilah, just you. Delilah represents the strange woman, but you are the chosen. The man of your dreams is looking for a woman who will enjoy the sexual experiences all the way into old age.

It is important to find out the true purpose for building a strong relationship. A woman who is marriage material has divorced her past and is now ready to receive all the good things the future holds for her. She is no longer bound by the mistakes of her past and her bad behaviors. Her thoughts have changed her behavior and her positive behavior has helped her receive good results. This is what you call harmony. Now you can be at peace with yourself and your future mate. This is who a man wants to marry -- a woman who can make his environment peaceful. She can turn a house into a home because she has virtue.

Relationships fail because of a lack of preparation. Let God prepare you for this next major season in your life. God is more concerned about the journey than the destination. There are some great tools that you will pick up during your singlehood that you can't gather when you are married. Becoming the woman he will love to marry requires being intentional, available and teachable. Your upcoming marriage can be a success story only if you want to put the prayer, preparation, and work into achieve this tremendous blessing.

What are some of the qualities you need to become marriage material?

_____
_____
_____
_____
_____
_____
_____
_____

How can I become a woman he would love to marry?

_____
_____
_____
_____
_____
_____
_____

Chapter 12

THE RIGHT MATE

There are so many books and materials available on avoiding the wrong mate but not enough on identifying the right mate. In this last chapter my goal is to help you recognize a good man when you see one. Many wounded women have a hard time distinguishing the bad from the good. All men have good and bad qualities, but there are some men who are marriage material. These are the types of men who are rare to find. However, now that you have gone through some of the healing processes in this book, your antennas might be a little more alert. Listed below are a few signs to let you know that you have met a potentially good mate.

1. Communication

If you feel comfortable being yourself around him and you guys are open, transparent, and honest with each other, this is a very good sign to keep pursuing the relationship.

2. Integrity

Does he follow through with the things he says that he will do? Is his word his bond? This is very important in relationships. Marriages have ended in divorce court for lack of integrity.

3. Happiness

Are you happy when you hear his name or does the thought of

him make you feel disgusted? Although happiness comes from within, Mr. Right should spark some type of happiness when you're together. You should feel like you are on top of the world because he's a part of your life. If you dread seeing him, this is not a good sign.

4. Spiritual

His relationship with God is the most important thing. If you are a believer, please make sure he is. Being unequally yoked can be very challenging.

5. Consideration

Does he care about what bothers you? Is the relationship one-sided or do you feel the same love that you give to him? Does he make you feel wanted? If you have to question the direction of the relationship often, then he has not considered you as a person in his future.

6. Stability

Mr. Right is stable physically, emotionally, spiritually and financially. He may not be rich or happy all the time but he can pay his bills and enjoys spending time with you. Emotionally mature men are healthy. This type of man is usually in touch with his own emotions and not up and down all the time. He's balanced. His spiritual walk is one of balance and consistency.

7. Responsible

A marriage material man doesn't have a problem with responsibilities. He pays his bills and cares for his children. He honors his commitments and takes joy in fulfilling his duties. He's a faithful man. He's ready for a permanent relationship.

Along with these seven important traits of Mr. Right, you want to make sure he is attractive. Being attractive is important but character is a priority. Handsome cannot carry you through life storms. You would need a little more than sex to handle the challenges of being married. Charm is good but it can also be deceitful. If he makes you happy, I'm sure humor and charm are somewhere in there.

Mr. Right is also ready for a relationship. You don't have to convince him to date you because he already knows what he wants. Once he has found you, he's not dating other women. He has had time to evaluate you and get to know your likes and dislikes as well as his own personal non-negotiables. The most important thing I want you to take from this book is to know yourself. Don't settle for less because you deserve God's best. Allow God to heal, refresh, and replenish your soul and the best is waiting for you.

How do I identify a good potential mate?

_____

_____

_____

_____

_____

_____

_____

What characteristics should he possess?

_____

_____

_____

_____

_____

_____

_____

About the Author

Elishia Dupree is a motivational speaker, prophetess, and life coach. Among her many titles, she is an established playwright, actress, and a real estate expert. She travels often speaking and conducting conferences nationally. Her greatest honor is being the mother of four handsome boys, Juvan, Greg, Steve and Deion.

Elishia has been active in ministry for roughly 14 years and has a passion to Inspire, Motivate and Empower people.

For other products and live events, visit us at: elishiadupree.org

48883677R00050

Made in the USA
Charleston, SC
14 November 2015